IMAGES
of America

OFFUTT
AIR FORCE BASE

ON THE COVER: Gen. Bruce K. Holloway, the sixth commander in chief of the Strategic Air Command (SAC), leans over the shoulder of a colonel in the SAC underground. Constructed between 1955 and 1957, approximately 1,000 people worked in the SAC underground during its peak. In the event of an emergency, the underground had the ability to sustain up to 800 people for a two-week period.

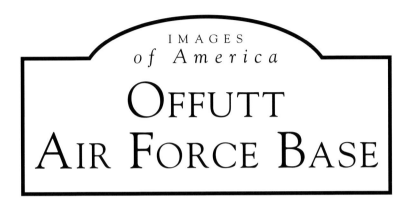

IMAGES
of America

OFFUTT
AIR FORCE BASE

Ben Justman of the Sarpy County Museum
Foreword by CMSAF (Ret.) James M. McCoy

ARCADIA
PUBLISHING

Published by Arcadia Publishing
Charleston, South Carolina

Printed in the United States of America

Library of Congress Control Number: 2014936383

For all general information, please contact Arcadia Publishing:
Telephone 843-853-2070
Fax 843-853-0044
E-mail sales@arcadiapublishing.com
For customer service and orders:
Toll-Free 1-888-313-2665

Visit us on the Internet at www.arcadiapublishing.com

This book is dedicated to the past, present, and future
servicemen and women of this nation.

CONTENTS

FOREWORD

In 1961, I was a young technical sergeant assigned to Air Force ROTC duty at the University of Notre Dame. During my first year at the detachment, I learned that my position had been eliminated due to a manpower study and that I was being reassigned to the 305th Bomber Wing (SAC) at Bunker Hill Air Force Base (now Grissom AFB), Indiana. Obviously, I was a very unhappy camper, since I did not want to leave Notre Dame and, further, did not want to be assigned to a SAC base. For a long time, I am sure there were heel marks along Highway 31 from South Bend to Bunker Hill. Little did I know at that time that, after 10 years, I would eventually be assigned to Offutt AFB after my tours at Bunker Hill and Barksdale Air Force Base, Louisiana, as Chief Master Sergeant of the Air Force.

After a successful tour at Hickam AFB, I was selected by Gen. Russell E. Dougherty, commander in chief of the Strategic Air Command, to become the first SAC senior enlisted advisor here at Offutt AFB once again. During my four years in this position, I went on to become the sixth Chief Master Sergeant of the Air Force, and then departed Offutt once again for the Pentagon in 1979. When I retired in 1981, we decided upon the Offutt area, returning to Bellevue, where we owned a home and became involved with the Bellevue/Omaha community.

During my military assignments at Offutt, I learned of the great significance and importance that the local communities around this base play in having this installation nearby. In 1995, I served on a committee to ensure that Offutt was not placed on the BRAC list of bases to be closed. At the same time, I learned of the historical importance Fort Crook has to Offutt AFB.

We are fortunate to have Ben Justman in our community, where he serves as the executive director of the Sarpy County Museum. This pictorial history book of Fort Crook/Offutt is well worth reading, offering a glimpse into the past; it will prove to be a useful resource in the future.

—James M. McCoy
Chief Master Sergeant of the Air Force (Ret)

James M. McCoy enlisted in the Air Force in January 1951. He became Chief Master Sergeant of the Air Force, the highest noncommissioned officer position, and served in that role from August 1979 to July 1981. McCoy retired on July 1, 1981, yet he has continued to remain very active in the Air Force community. Today, the James M. McCoy Airman Leadership School at Offutt is named in his honor.

ACKNOWLEDGMENTS

Support for this book has been graciously provided by the 55th Wing, Michael Bellis, Connie Crow, John and Donna Daly, Bill Doyle, Mary Langhorst, James McCoy, Donita Mitchell, Jim and Pat Peaker, Dorene Sherman, Donald Shook, Sissy Silber, Michael Wagner, and the board of directors of the Sarpy County Museum. Unless otherwise noted, all images appear courtesy of the Sarpy County Museum.

—Ben Justman
Executive Director, Sarpy County Museum

INTRODUCTION

The legacy of Offutt Air Force Base begins long before there was an Air Force, before the first motorized heavier-than-air flight, before modern rocketry, and, certainly, before the first programmable electric computer. It was, in a way, a simpler time, and yet the world of 1888 was a complex and fragile one. That year, plans were laid for the future military post in Sarpy County, Nebraska, not far from the Missouri River. It gained a name, Fort Crook, in 1891, following the death of Maj. Gen. George Crook, who had been a West Point graduate and 38-year veteran of the Army. Construction and planning took several years, and it was not until 1896 that the fort transformed from the Nebraska plain to a state-of-the-art late-19th-century US military installation. The *Omaha Daily Bee* went as far as calling it the "finest and most conveniently arranged post in the United States Army."

The fort received its first tests when its men went off to Cuba during the Spanish-American War and, later, to the Philippines. Many men returned. Some did not. It again encountered the winds of war during World War I, where the most famous casualty associated with the fort actually had no firsthand physical connection at all. American pilot Jarvis Offutt lost his life during World War I. In 1924, a small flying field was erected at Fort Crook and named in his honor.

By December 7, 1941, a date that lives in infamy, Fort Crook had become a well-oiled machine, ready to help bring the war to an end just as America had entered it. The Glenn L. Martin Company had utilized the base to construct an aircraft production facility. The Martin bomber plant at Fort Crook is one of the quintessential home front narratives of World War II. Workers there built more than 2,000 bombers. Their efforts aided in bringing about an end to the war quite literally: the pair of modified B-29 bombers that dropped the atomic bombs over Japan were both constructed and customized at Fort Crook.

The year 1948 brought about the biggest historical change to the post. The Army flag was lowered, and, on January 13, 1948, the newly sewn US Air Force flag was raised. Fort Crook was no more. Offutt Air Force Base was now on the map. While the change was smooth and seamless, it presumably took more than a change-of-address form to complete the process. The transformation could be argued as inevitable, with Offutt's deep history of aviation, but this was in the years immediately following World War II. The US military had reached an apex in May 1945 with eight million personnel. By 1948, that number had dwindled to less than 550,000. At war's end, most men went home, married their sweetheart, had children, forgot about the war, and worked hard to enter the serene fairy-tale life of the 1950s. Offutt, like so many other American military installations that did their duty during those tumultuous years, could have simply shuttered up overnight.

However, Offutt did not melt away into civilian life. The Soviet Union ensured that. Rather, it faced a new challenge to peace and stability in this country and abroad. "From Stettin in the Baltic to Trieste in the Adriatic, an iron curtain has descended across the continent" of Europe, Winston Churchill stated in his now-famous speech.

The same year the Air Force assumed command, Offutt became home to Strategic Air Command. SAC became a fixture not just within the military community but also within American culture during the Cold War years. The role of Offutt grew in size and scope during this time. The Air Force Weather Agency, Looking Glass Operations, National Emergency Airborne Command, 3902d Air Base, 55th Wing and other units have all had a role in that. To accommodate the influx, entire new housing developments dedicated to airmen and their families were constructed. Yet it could all have disappeared in the blink of an eye had nuclear deterrence failed. By 1992, with America's adversary in checkmate, SAC stood down. The United States Strategic Command, a new command with a new role and mission, stepped up.

Today, Offutt Air Force Base has greatly changed from its early days as Fort Crook, when the newspaper bragged of a wagon road to connect the 10-mile distance between the fort and Omaha. It has gone from a base of a few hundred men to a combined military and civilian workforce of over 10,000. However, there is a crucial main artery of continuity throughout the entire timeframe: national defense. Offutt Air Force Base has, does, and always will continue to serve in the defense of this nation and its allies in order to help promote global peace.

The saying goes, "Once you get Offutt, you never get off it." Offutt can be a place where men and women spend two or three years in their military careers or it can be a place where they stay for the near duration. Either way, the experiences at Offutt have shaped countless individuals, communities, and this country as a whole. It is a very active institution with a vital mission, but also one with a deep tradition and a rich past, much of which has been included within this book.

The majority of the photographs in this volume can be found within the archives at the Sarpy County Museum, and, unless otherwise noted, they are courtesy of the museum's collection. Further images stem from the office of the 55th Wing historian, various regimental historical organizations, and generous community members. This book can only begin to draw upon the nearly 125-year history of Offutt AFB. There are many more images and stories out there. They are put away in the attic, basement, closet, or deep within the mind. Please consider sharing with the Sarpy County Museum so the history of Offutt can be shared for generations.

Taken from the skies on August 30, 1927, this is the future home of Offutt AFB, known at the time as Fort Crook, an Army post surrounded by farmland despite being only 10 miles from Omaha. That year, Fort Crook was described as "the Midwest center of reserve training activities" by the *Omaha World Herald*.

One

OLD ARMY POST

THE EARLY YEARS

The story of Fort Crook (present-day Offutt Air Force Base) does not begin in Nebraska. Instead, it can be traced to a bill on Capitol Hill, introduced by Nebraska senator Charles F. Manderson in December 1887. The bill permitted the secretary of war to sell Fort Omaha assets and purchase land suitable for a new military installation. Pres. Grover Cleveland signed the bill into law on July 23, 1888.

Opened in 1869, Fort Omaha, originally named Sherman Barracks, was deemed too small to function as an effective military post. At 82.5 acres, it allowed for administrative duties and parade ground maneuvers but suffered limitations to train soldiers for conflict. Even after its closure, Fort Omaha would rematerialize in specialized roles throughout the years. In 1975, Metropolitan Community College established its campus on 70 acres of the former fort.

Authorization to build the fort was limited to "not more than 1,000 acres in Sarpy, Washington, or Douglas County." Ultimately, a site near the little village of Bellevue was chosen. The first land was purchased in 1889, a tract consisting of 502.59 acres bought for $61,400, or $122.17 per acre. A further 43.08 acres were purchased that same year, bringing the total to 545.67 acres.

Construction of Officers' Row began in 1891 under the direction of Capt. Charles Frederick Humphrey. After rising from the rank of private, Humphrey would later retire a major general, quartermaster of the Army in 1907. Prior to overseeing the construction, Humphrey received the Medal of Honor for his actions during the Indian Wars.

Quarters 1–12 of Officers' Row were constructed first and were completed by October 1894. Each structure was built as a duplex billet for two families. Quarters 14, 15, and 19–24 were completed in the spring of 1894. Unlike the other buildings on the row, made of brick, the final structures, Quarters 25–28, were wooden-framed and were completed in March 1898.

Officers Row.   Fort Crook, Neb.

The officers' mess and club, Quarters 13, was completed in November 1895. Aspects of the original building included a kitchen, reading room, and billiards room. Additionally, Quarters 13 housed the bachelor quarters, with accommodations for eight single officers. Today, it functions as a meeting spot for small gatherings and as lodging for distinguished visitors to Offutt.

The brick duplex homes on Officers' Row each contain a parlor, dining room, kitchen with a pantry, four bedrooms on the second floor, and servants' quarters on the top floor. The rooms were finished with oak and were heated by steam from a coal fire. Each duplex building was built at a cost of $17,500.

The new fort gained a name on March 3, 1891, in honor of the late Maj. Gen. George Crook, veteran of the Indian Wars and the Civil War. Friend and foe equally respected Crook. The Apache dubbed him "Grey Wolf," while Pres. Rutherford B. Hayes named his own son George Crook Hayes. Despite his actions on the battlefield, where he fought Crazy Horse and Geronimo, among others, Crook spent his later years speaking out against the ill treatment of Native Americans. In 1879, he testified on behalf of the Ponca Tribe during the trial of Standing Bear, where a federal judge determined that an Indian was due the rights and privileges of man. While still in uniform, Crook passed away suddenly at the age of 61. Both Gene Hackman and Peter Coyote have portrayed Crook in film and television productions.

The buildings have largely retained their original traits, despite several modernizing updates. The homes gained electricity in 1905, when the entire post was connected to the grid. The coal fires to create steam heat were switched over to gas furnaces in 1950–1951. While the bathroom fixtures, complete with claw-foot tubs, remained, the original plumbing did not. It was finally overhauled in 1954–1955. Air conditioning was installed in 1967–1968.

The remaining unique building on the row, Quarters 16 was constructed for the commanding officer and is the only single residence on Officers' Row. Built at a cost of $10,989 and finished in September 1896, the 34-foot-by-54-foot structure was home to the post commander's residence until 1948. It then became home to the commander in chief of SAC. Today, the commander of the US Strategic Command and his family occupy the dwelling.

Five years may seem like a long time to build a smattering of buildings, but the quartermaster corps had to take into account freshwater wells, sewer systems, roads, and building materials, all of which had to be thought out in great detail prior to the arrival of the first garrison troops.

Those garrison troops first arrived with an advance party of 10 enlisted men, led by 2nd Lt. David Stanley of Company C, 22nd Infantry Regiment, on a warm summer day in late June 1896. Nine days later, Col. James S. Casey arrived to take command. This photograph of Company H of the 22nd features a number of noncommissioned officers (NCOs), privates, and even the company bugler. (Courtesy of Michael Bellis, 22nd Infantry Regiment Society.)

The blacksmith shop was the first building completed at Fort Crook in 1893. The structure was used not only by blacksmiths but also by a variety of other tradesmen. Work would have been labor-intensive, similar to what is seen in this photograph of the fort's steam-heating plant. At one time, the blacksmith shop had four large doors, in similar fashion to modern-day service bays, only instead of vehicles, these were for animals.

Not just reserved for cavalry units, four-legged animals were essential to haul anything the regular infantryman could not carry on his back, especially if rail transport was not an option. During the Civil War, one animal was required for every 3.75 men, while in World War I, approximately one animal for every four men was needed. In a true show of modernization, the old stables at Fort Crook were torn down, and the area is now a parking lot.

The guardhouse was one of the early buildings constructed at the fort. It was used to confine men for minor offenses. One of these men, Samuel Morgan of the 8th Cavalry, was held at the guardhouse for desertion. On November 17, 1898, Morgan and another prisoner subdued the guard on duty and escaped. Morgan was chased to nearby La Platte and was killed in the ensuing exchange. In the aftermath, a court-martial was held for the two men who killed Morgan. Found not guilty of manslaughter, they were promptly arrested on the order of a Sarpy County judge and held on bail of $1,000 each. The matter was ultimately resolved, but it was a significant enough event to gain the attention of Elihu Root, the secretary of war. This jail, now known as confinement, is still used for its original purpose.

The barracks were built as one block-long building with residential wings on either side of a central area that included dining and recreational facilities. At the turn of the 20th century, the base surgeon commented that there were 1,379 men present, totaling 12 over-strength companies, even though the building was intended for only eight companies. Overcrowding was alleviated, albeit temporarily, by billeting men in the attic of the building.

The central portion included a bowling alley. In December 1946, a fire started there. A valiant effort by military and civilian firefighters from Bellevue put out the fire, limiting damage to the central area. The two residential wings were saved. Where one long building once stood on the east side of the parade grounds, there are now two buildings with a space between them.

Similar to Officers' Row but smaller and with less pomp, the noncommissioned officers' row, situated on the parade ground, served as home for a number of senior sergeants and their families. The row consisted of 12 two-bedroom homes and one two-story unit for the junior NCOs. Known officially today as Prestige Chief Housing, the buildings still retain their original function, but the units have been remodeled as single-family homes.

Fort Crook was not a shady place. A June 1896 *Omaha World Herald* article mentioned that a number of small cottonwood trees were recently planted to supplement the few maple and box elder trees located in the southern region of the fort. It went on to say that the grounds were covered "with native sand grass and a few acres of clover on the south side of the hospital hill."

Built at a distance from the rest of the fort to safeguard against contagious disease, the hospital was a blessing for military personnel. In a close call, the roof was torn off in the 1908 tornado. Fortunately, there was enough time to get everyone to the basement and no one was seriously hurt. The post hospital was torn down in 1940 to make room for the Martin bomber plant.

Capt. Dr. William B. Banister served as the first assistant surgeon at Fort Crook until August 1897. Banister, later promoted to major and then colonel, eventually found himself in the thick of the Chinese Boxer Rebellion as chief surgeon of the China Relief Expedition in 1900. Colonel Banister retired in 1922 after 36 years in the military and retired to Nebraska to open up a private practice.

The regimental band could commonly be found on the parade ground. When they were not, they were practicing in their own quarters, isolated from the rest of the troops to keep their cacophonous noise to a minimum. The band quarters, similar to numerous other structures, were torn down in preparation for the construction of the Martin bomber plant. No new band quarters were built in their place.

While soldiers were not soldiering, there were other diversions available for periods of leisure. The American pastime, baseball, was popular with troops; a baseball diamond was installed in 1905. The Fort Crook team would square off against local town teams such as those in Bellevue and Papillion.

The nearby town of Fort Crook, located just outside the main gate, offered a full selection of saloons, restaurants, and other stores that primarily catered to servicemen. Judging by the requests for liquor licenses, saloons outnumbered other businesses. In 1900, the community thrived with a population of 646, but, following tornados, floods, fires, and laws hindering the sale of alcohol, the population had dwindled to just 203 by 1910.

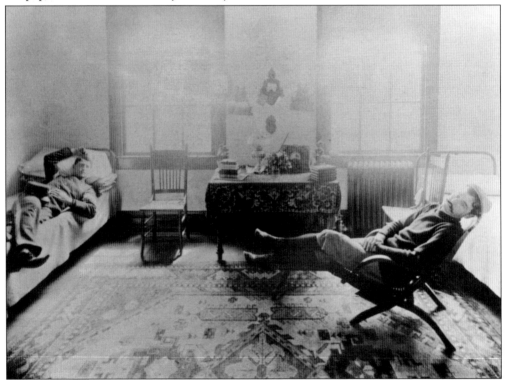

A pair of NCOs relax in their quarters around 1900. Duties and responsibilities of the era were long, hard, and dirty, but there were civilized comforts in their billet. If one was not interested in baseball, the sins offered in town, or the handful of other activities, there was always the opportunity to simply rest and read up. (Courtesy of Offutt Air Force Base.)

The men of the 22nd Infantry did not have a lackadaisical lifestyle while at Fort Crook. Sure, there was time for diversions, but there was also ample opportunity for marching and training. In September 1897, the 22nd marched round-trip to Schuyler, Nebraska, approximately 110 miles total. Temperatures were recorded at 100 degrees. This image shows the rear guard and wagon train during that march.

Marching in the field could be exhausting. In 1905 and 1906, the 30th Infantry Regiment at Fort Crook went on marches that were over 200 miles and could last for several weeks. The soldier was forced to do without the creature comforts of the fort while in the field. However, as is apparent from this image, they still managed to do rather well for themselves. (Courtesy of Offutt Air Force Base.)

The men of Company C, 22nd Infantry, practice on the Fort Crook rifle range. It was noted that they practiced firing at 300 yards and that the crack of rifles filled the air during training. There is at least one documented instance of a nearby farmer's horse being shot. It is likely that many of the men pictured here were engaged in combat during the Spanish-American War.

Col. Charles A. Wikoff (first row, fifth from left) assumed command of the 22nd at Fort Crook on January 28, 1897. During his time at the fort, Wikoff resided in Quarters 16 of Officers' Row. Popular with the 22nd, he relinquished his command after landing in Cuba. Shortly after, he was mortally wounded during the battle of San Juan Hill. He was the most senior American officer to die during the Spanish-American War. (Courtesy of Michael Bellis, 22nd Infantry Regiment Society.)

Cpl. John L. Evans, Company H, 22nd Infantry, poses for a professional photographer. The studio of William H. McKay of Omaha took many of the images of early Fort Crook. The rifles are .30-caliber Krag Jorgensen rifles, the standard rifle of the Army prior to the M1903 Springfield. (Courtesy of Michael Bellis, 22nd Infantry Regiment Society.)

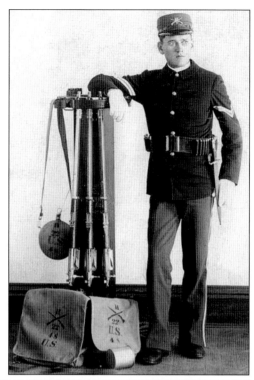

The 22nd Infantry arrived by train with their families in 1896. Once the Spanish-American War broke out in 1898, the 22nd would be deployed to Cuba and, later, to the Philippines. During the 22nd's interim stay at Fort Crook between deployments, a number of soldiers suffered from tropical diseases. Six men were buried on the base cemetery between September 1898 and January 1899. Many more never returned to Nebraska.

Following the departure of the 22nd Infantry to Cuba, Fort Crook suddenly found itself empty again. Only 41 enlisted men and two officers, the senior of them being a first lieutenant, remained at the fort. Wives and families also stayed behind at Fort Crook. Here, men of Company D, 22nd Infantry, including Ed Reynolds (fourth from right), demonstrate a variety of different uniforms. (Courtesy of the Reynolds family.)

The firing of a six-pound field gun on the parade ground was a daily routine at Fort Crook to announce reveille and retreat, as this photograph from around 1905 shows through the smoke. The tradition has since ceased, but several replica cannons remain on the parade ground today, near the gazebo.

The enlisted men in the barracks did not have private suites. They shared a common billeting area. They would awaken for reveille to a bugler's call and assemble on the parade ground for roll call. The flag would be raised, and the cannon sounded. A man on his first enlistment at Fort Crook around 1907 earned $13 per month and had his housing, uniform, and meals provided.

Q.M. Sgt. Herman Coffman poses in front of his residence. Coffman was the ranking man when he assumed command of the post in March 1913. All able-bodied troops and officers departed for duty in Texas. Once there, they would take part in the punitive expedition into Mexico against Pancho Villa. (Courtesy of Offutt Air Force Base.)

Parked on the dirt road in front of Generals' Row, the press corps anxiously awaited the arrival of secretary of war and presidential candidate William Howard Taft. The visit took place on April 6, 1908, and did not last long. Taft's chief opponent for the office of president was the Nebraskan William Jennings Bryan. Following a brief reception for Taft and photograph opportunity on the porch at Quarters 16, the procession made its way through the rain to Council Bluffs in a mere 28 minutes. (Both courtesy of the Bostwick-Frohardt Collection, KM3TV; on permanent loan to the Durham Museum.)

Two

TO THE SKIES
AIR POWER AND INTERWAR YEARS

The first air unit assigned to Fort Crook did not even have airplanes. The 61st Balloon Company arrived at Fort Crook on September 10, 1918. Their role was not combat, but observation. One month later the war ended, and the 61st was demobilized, never making it to Europe. Of the 110 balloon companies in the US Signal Corps, only 35 ever actually made it overseas.

Born in Omaha on October 26, 1894, 1st Lt. Jarvis Offutt was one of 300 American flyers trained in Canada and attached to the Royal Air Force. Offutt was an active student and always sought challenges. Prior to transferring to aviation, he was involved with artillery units and served as the company supply sergeant while at Yale. He received his officer commission as a first lieutenant in the aviation section of the Army Signal Corps. Tragically, Offutt was killed while ferrying airplanes from factories in England to their bases in France on August 13, 1918. The Fort Crook landing field was named Offutt Field in his honor on May 10, 1924. In 1948, Fort Crook was redesignated Offutt Air Force Base.

In the spring of 1921, construction was completed on the first permanent steel hangar to accompany two dirt runways; the longer of them measured 2,640 feet long. Among the first aircraft were two DeHaviland DH-4 and two Curtis Jenny biplanes, utilized primarily for US Postal Service airmail delivery. In May 1924, the flying field of Fort Crook was designated Offutt Field.

This action shot captures the filming of Lt. Erik Nelson landing his Douglas DT-2 at Fort Crook's recently christened Offutt Field. In 1924, Nelson was part of the team that achieved the first aerial circumnavigation of the globe. The trip took 175 days and covered 27,553 miles. Of interesting note is the sabre worn by the officer fifth from the left. (Courtesy of Offutt Air Force Base.)

In the summer of 1925, the US Postal Service completed a 10-plane hangar. Airmail service for Omaha and the surrounding area was flown in and out of Fort Crook for the next five years. Despite the investment in infrastructure at Fort Crook, airmail service was transferred to the Omaha Municipal Airport in 1930.

Almost all of the first 14 years of Maj. E.W. Crockett's career was spent in the Philippines. In February 1918, he reported to Fort Omaha with the Aviation Section, Signal Corps. In September his unit was transferred to Fort Crook, where he served as the first commander of the first air unit to the post. Despite serving a number of different roles in the Philippines, the major was a pilot at Fort Crook.

Be it air or land, mechanization filtered into Fort Crook. Archaic by modern standards, the Nash Quad was popular around the time of World War I. The four-wheel-drive hauler was more expensive than other vehicles of the day, but was cheaper than the Army mule. Although, with a maximum speed of 15 miles per hour, the Nash Quad may not have been much faster.

A low-level flight over the flying field demonstrates the entire early splendor, showing the tower, two hangars, and maintenance and administrative buildings. To help improve safety, the US Weather Bureau had a presence on the post. By 1925, the DeHaviland DH-4 was replaced with the new Douglas M-1 single-seat biplane.

Charles Lindbergh's famous New York–Paris flight in May 1927 made him an American hero. Fresh in the limelight, Lindbergh visited Omaha on August 30, 1927. Despite not landing at Offutt Field, there is no question that the public image of the pilot had obtained movie star–like status. (Courtesy of the Bostwick-Frohardt Collection, KM3TV; on permanent loan to the Durham Museum.)

An aerial shot from 1931 displays Fort Crook in its interwar splendor. A far cry from the Air Force base it evolved into, the baseball diamond is perhaps its largest visible feature. Other aspects of the fort include the peaked white tents situated on the parade ground. In the distance beyond the diamond is the small airfield known as Offutt Field.

In 1930, the first large-scale training was held for reserve pilots of the Seventh Corps Area. Additionally, planes were flown in from Marshall Army Air Field at Fort Riley in Kansas for the event. A group of 25 pilots practiced formation flying, bombing runs, aerial machine-gunnery, and advanced aeronautics. Twin-engine bombers, while not rare, were unique and fulfilled a special role.

In 1927, the post office contracted its airmail services at Fort Crook to the Boeing Air Transport Corporation. They were permitted to fly in and out of Offutt and use the brick hangar during their services. In 1929, the work was also farmed out to the Robertson Aircraft Company. After operations folded at Fort Crook, Robertson would eventually merge with half a dozen other companies to form American Airlines.

The second steel hangar at Fort Crook was 66 feet by 104 feet. The lowest bid to construct the building was submitted at $7,800; however, the War Department declined this offer, citing it as far too costly. Instead, it was constructed internally, using soldiers to build the hangar. The cost allotted to construct the building by the War Department was far lower than the bid, only $500.

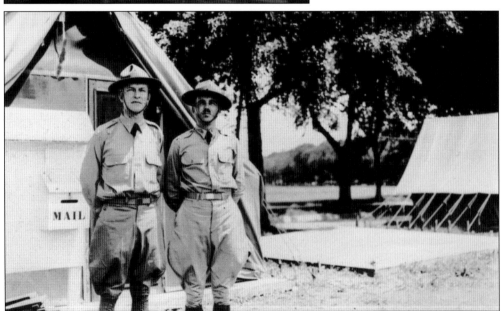

Col. Paul Bliss (left) and Captain Erickson, adjutant of the Corps Area Service Command during the summer of 1936, are seen here. During this era, exercises were geared towards the experiences and situations of the last war, not the next. The service command was headquartered in Nebraska at Fort Crook, but the region included Arkansas, Kansas, Minnesota, Missouri, North and South Dakota, and Iowa. (Courtesy of Offutt Air Force Base.)

Members of the 17th Infantry are shown here in September 1931 with various trophies. Two of the awards are for bowling and another is for "championship" marksmanship. The commanding officer of the 17th, Col. LaVergne Greeg, the only man wearing a Sam Browne belt, sits squarely in the middle of the first row.

The 17th Infantry Band is seen here in their best with their families at what was probably a Christmas celebration in 1934. The photograph nicely displays the band quarters, which shared a common appearance with the rest of the Fort Crook historic district. Fort Crook had three different post commanders in three consecutive months during that year: Maj. Kenneth Hanst, Col. Thomas Anderson, and Col. Samuel Sutherland, in September, October, and November, respectively.

Band, 17th Infantry, Ft. Crook, Neb., June 1938. Capt. Cc
W.O. *William J. Bale*

Up until their quarters were torn down, the band was a mainstay at Fort Crook. In June 1938, the 17th Infantry Band put on their best crisp, clean uniforms and polished their brass for this photograph on the parade ground. The band played not only for formal functions such as change of command ceremonies, but also for galas and community celebrations, such as one in October 1935 in McCook, Nebraska. Wilford Bright, on the slide trombone, to the immediate left of the

Commanding

drummer, continued to serve through World War II, though much of that time was not spent at Fort Crook. It is easy to suspect that the band probably had a number of Big Band favorites in their repertoire, including Benny Goodman's "Sing, Sing, Sing," which had come out a year prior, in 1937.

Camaraderie has always been an important morale-boosting factor. The 17th Infantry celebrated Organization Day in May 1931. The Army tradition is a day of food, fun, and often family. Athletic competitions were held throughout the morning, there was a barbecue for lunch and a movie in the afternoon, and the day concluded with an enlisted men's dance at 9:00 p.m. The celebration included a 36-page commemorative booklet highlighting the regimental history.

Benjamin Lewis Holt (circled, second row, left) is pictured here with his Citizens' Military Training Camp (CMTC) class, which came to Fort Crook for the program in 1935. Perhaps it was the CMTC that encouraged him to enlist in the Navy a few years later, and he attended boot camp in 1937. From 1938 through most of the war, he served aboard the battleship USS *Idaho*, eventually retiring from the Navy in 1947. (Courtesy of the Holt family.)

Citizens' Military Training Camp (CMTC) was a national military training program created under the National Defense Act of 1920 and held during the summers of 1921 through 1940. The program was designed to allow civilians an opportunity to explore military training in a monthlong program. One such camp was held at Fort Crook beginning in 1927. The men of CMTC were mostly between the ages of 17 and 24. Senior supervision was by the men of the 17th Infantry at Fort Crook, while immediate command was usually by members of college ROTC programs or men of the infantry reserve. The Fort Crook CMTC program had four companies, each with approximately 140 men. The total number of candidates at the camp in 1927 was 641.

Nebraska and the nation were facing tough economic times during the Great Depression years. One of Pres. Franklin D. Roosevelt's New Deal programs, the Civilian Conservation Corps (CCC), attempted to alleviate economic hardships by putting Americans to work. Beginning in 1933, Fort Crook was the Nebraska–South Dakota regional headquarters of the CCC. The CCC personnel were isolated from regular military personnel, so they had a separate mess hall, barracks, and other facilities. With different organization and discipline, there may have been some strife between Army and CCC personnel. This is highlighted by the fact that, in 1934, an Army private drew $17.85 per month, while his CCC counterpart earned $30 per month. Despite their better pay and undoubtedly better food, the CCC would not last, moving from their Fort Crook facilities in 1937.

Christmas can be a difficult time for a member of the armed forces. In spite of the Great Depression, the men at Fort Crook were still treated to a very fine meal on Christmas in 1931. Dinner included roast turkey and baked ham, snowflake potatoes, sweet potatoes, shrimp salad, stuffed olives, mincemeat pie, and sugar, cigarettes, and cigars for desert. It is unconfirmed if they had leftovers for December 26.

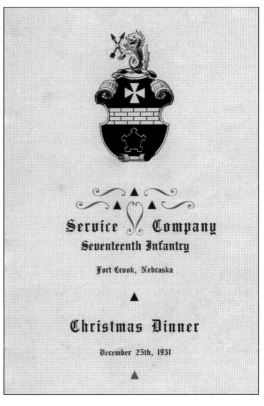

Service Company
Seventeenth Infantry

Fort Crook, Nebraska

Christmas Dinner

December 25th, 1931

The base commander's tenure is often short, usually two to three years on average. Col. Clyde R. Abraham assumed command of the 17th Infantry at Fort Crook on October 5, 1936, and was only in command at the post until December 3, 1938. During that time, however, the 17th became motorized, the CCC moved off post, floodlights were installed on the runway, and a new 125-man barracks was commissioned. (Courtesy of Donald Shook, 17th Infantry Regiment Association.)

On March 3, 1937, the service club, a home away from home for many, was gutted by fire. Built at a cost of $11,000 in 1917, the club was an important focal point during the interwar years for many on-base happenings. Had the service club not burned down, in all probability, it would have been torn down to make way for the bomber plant as the threat of war drew closer.

For those looking to take in a motion picture, a theater was built at a cost of $27,000 in 1933, the height of the Great Depression. The one-story building has a mezzanine and a projection booth. This 1936 photograph shows a crew of men shoveling the walkways. The theater was used well into the 1990s and is listed in the National Register of Historic Places.

Built in 1933 at an approximate cost of $3,500, these elaborate gardens could be found directly behind Officers' Row. Reports are conflicting, with some claiming that the gardens were actually built by the CCC. If so, this would have been a prohibited use of federal funds for a military-related project. Whether someone was court-martialed as a result remains unclear. Either way, the bulk of the gardens were leveled in 1941.

William Little poses in front of the Fort Crook gate in 1939. The gate was little more than a roadway with two brick pillars, a far cry from the historical evolution of the base gates through the years. Security was not just lax; it was nearly nonexistent. In fact, guards were not posted to check identification until after World War II. (Courtesy of the Little family.)

The gate is seen here during a visit by an unknown general, as Col. Clyde R. Abraham greets him. The great divide between Army post and open land is not much. In the background, several buildings of the town of Fort Crook are seen. Once booming, it was quite sleepy by the 1930s. (Courtesy of Donald Shook, 17th Infantry Regiment Association.)

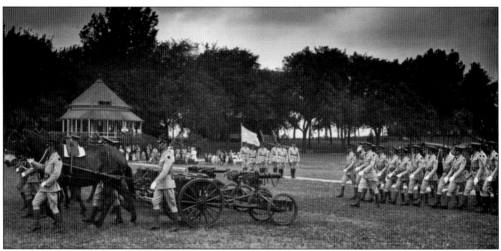

The situation was already volatile in Asia and Europe when this photograph of the 17th was taken at Fort Crook in 1938. Of interesting note are the horse- and mule-drawn units. The wagons, which hauled machine guns for the regiment, emphasize the woefully primitive position the United States was in as worldwide hostilities were about to boil over. (Courtesy of Donald Shook, 17th Infantry Regiment Association.)

Three

WEATHER THE STORM
THE WAR YEARS

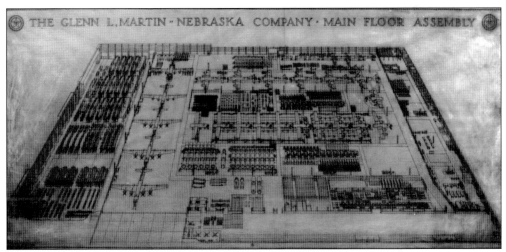

In December 1940, England stood alone in the battle for Europe. Brutal fighting raged in China. With the world in flames, America was not sitting idle. Instead, it was preparing for the inevitable. In January 1941, the Martin Company of Baltimore leased a large portion of Fort Crook from the US government. Their plan was to quickly construct a major airplane production facility.

The project called for the construction of nine buildings, including the assembly plant, now known as Building D. Before the first building could come up, several needed to come down. The original hospital, six units of officers' quarters, the band quarters, the CCC camp, the NCO club, and the golf course were all leveled in preparation for the bomber facilities and the new runway.

A significant amount of land was needed to accommodate the bomber plant facilities. In 1941, 503.85 acres were leased to the Martin-Nebraska Bomber Company. An additional 96.06 acres were purchased to expand the fort, bringing the total plant site to 641.76 acres. This was the majority of the installation, and 137.91 acres more than what was originally obtained to build Fort Crook in 1889.

The sheer amount of material to construct the assembly plant is amazing: 250 miles of electrical wiring was installed, 47,000 cubic yards of concrete were poured, 10 million square feet of paint was applied, 5 acres of glass was installed, and 10 miles of fluorescent lighting was installed. If the building seemed large, it is because it was. The floor space measured at 1.2 million square feet, or the equivalent of 25 full-sized football fields.

Equally impressive were the 2,500 workers employed in construction operations. Peter Kiewit Sons of nearby Omaha was awarded the contract and led the construction, with numerous other subcontractors and Kiewit associates to assist in the project. Collectively, they worked in three round-the-clock shifts to complete the project as soon as possible.

Shown clearly in this image is the flooring. Not just any surface, the flooring at the assembly plant was comprised of wooden blocks dipped in creosote and oil. This was said to make the shifting of machinery easier and to provide extra support to plant workers who were required to be stationary for long periods of time.

In late June 1941, the first steel beam was placed into position in the bomber assembly plant. Just 10 days later, the first contract for the production of 1,200 B-26C Marauders was received. That same month, Building A, the personnel building, was started. While the planes were constructed and modified in larger buildings, Building A is where the business decisions were made.

Nelson Drive serves as one of the main arteries of Offutt Air Force Base. Naval aviation cadet Robert Nelson, a Nebraska native, was killed on April 29, 1941, while piloting his plane over the Florida Everglades. With more than 1,000 people in attendance braving the cold weather, the street dedication ceremony at Fort Crook took place on December 7, 1941, just hours before the attack on Pearl Harbor.

The *Martin Star*, the monthly publication for the Martin Bomber Company, offered insights into wartime development, including the Nebraska plant at Fort Crook. Highlights of the publication include emphasis on Martin's airplanes, production notes, and profiles of plant workers. Occasionally, the Nebraska plant became the focus for entire articles. For example, this January 1943 issue included the article "Nebraska Women Learn to Build Bombers Quickly."

A number of the B-26C bombers built at Martin-Nebraska were actually given to America's allies. For example, the aircraft on the right was transferred to the Royal Air Force, which it ultimately retired from in May 1945. Other aircraft built at the plant were given to the French and South African Air Forces. The plane on the left remained a part of the Army Air Force operations and was scrapped in 1945.

With 14,527 persons employed, the plant reached its peak employment in November 1943. Production was not maintained around the clock; however, it did operate in three shifts, 22.5 hours a day, six days a week. November also brought about the completion of the 1,200 B-26 bombers. This accomplishment marked the end of the initial contract, first awarded to Martin-Nebraska in 1941.

All the effort paid off when, on December 13, 1943, Martin-Nebraska was awarded the Army-Navy "E" Production Award for their herculean efforts of operation on schedule for 12 consecutive months. The "E" stood for excellence. Another award was given in June 1944 for 18 consecutive months of on-schedule production, and a third and final "E" award was given in January 1945 for 24 months of on-schedule production.

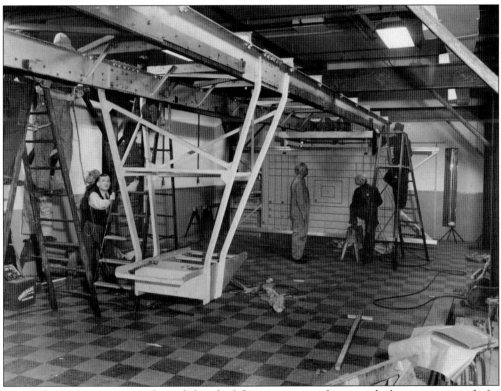

Personal cameras were strictly prohibited; if they were even discovered, they were grounds for termination. Smoking except in designated areas was also prohibited. Employees were not permitted to enter the plant more than 30 minutes prior to their start time. The Martin-Nebraska security guards were very thorough in their work. While personal cameras were forbidden, the room seen here still under construction did eventually contain a large camera utilized for blueprints.

Tragedy struck on September 22, 1943, when a B-25 crashed into the assembly plant, tearing a 75-foot hole into the roof and raining an explosive hellfire below. Three of the four crewmen aboard the B-25 were killed. The fourth miraculously survived, and even visited the crash site several months later. Even more incredible is that they were the only casualties. Most of the employees were away on lunch break at the time of the incident.

Not only was time of the essence, but cost of materials was as well. While a simple screw cost only a penny, it all added up. There were those at the plant whose entire job consisted of sorting nuts and bolts. The approximate cost per unit for a B-26 was $102,659. The cost per unit for a B-29 was significantly more, at $639,188.

The final B-26 Marauder rolled off the assembly line on April 4, 1944. Seen here, it saw action in Europe with the 495th Bombardment Squadron. It was a mark of triumph, the last of 1,585 to be produced at Fort Crook. Putting a damper on that accomplishment, this final B-26 crash-landed and burst into flames while returning from a mission on August 25, 1944. All crew were killed.

Two days after the final B-26 rolled off the assembly line, production of the first B-29 Superfortress began. That plane, 42-6229, found its way to India after its completion in May 1944. Martin-Nebraska was only one of four plants churning out B-29s that were ready for the front line. The other three facilities were in Atlanta, Wichita, and Renton, Washington.

Women playing wartime sports was not just a Hollywood tale told by Madonna and Rosie O'Donnell. The Martin-Nebraska Bomberettes were in "a league of their own," playing softball throughout the region and the country, but, as seen here, skirts were not part of the uniform. There was a men's team as well. One year, the men's team even made it to the national championship, held in Detroit.

Donita Gottsch, Bill Gayer, Walter Weddle, and Louise Tolander of the surface group set a new record in completing an aileron assembly. The aileron is what helps control the plane in flight and is found on the wings of fixed-wing aircraft such as the B-26 and B-29. Normally, the job took 24 hours and three shifts, but this group completed a finished aileron in just eight hours.

This was a reminder to the men and women at Martin-Nebraska as to what they were working for: the remains of a German fighter and field artillery piece on display at the southwest end of the plant's final assembly. The B-26 in the background, 42-107573, went on to avoid German fighters, completing 61 combat missions. Unfortunately, the other B-26 with a visible serial number, 42-107574, was shot down shortly after D-Day.

G.T. Wiley, vice president and general manager of Martin-Nebraska, and J.T. Hartson, executive vice president of the Glenn L. Martin Company, broke ground for the plant annexation in the summer of 1943. The $2 million project added 135,000 square feet to operations. At the height of the turning tide of the war, approval for the project cut through red tape and bureaucracy in a mere five days.

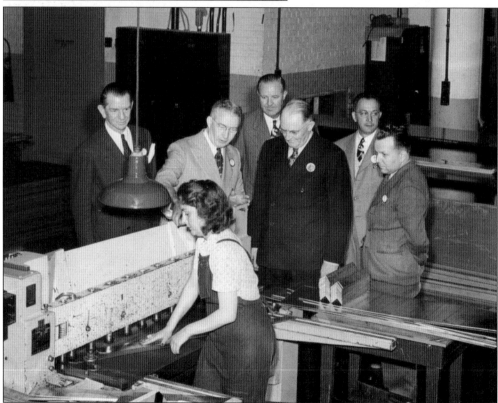

Glenn L. Martin, president of the company and its namesake, along with a number of high-ranking Martin executives, toured the plant. Here, they observe Ruth Robb of the first shift operating a shearing machine to press and cut sheet metal, a dangerous job if one was not careful.

Working on bombers was not enough. Employees at Martin-Nebraska also contributed money to the war effort, with different departments competing to generate the most funds. Different companies throughout the country also sponsored aircraft. The Maytag Corporation of Newton, Iowa, for example, paid for a B-26, the "Maytag Marauder," to be built. In fact, the exhaust systems for the B-26 were built in Newton and then sent to Fort Crook.

On April 26, 1943, President Roosevelt visited the bomber plant to get a firsthand view of the "arsenal of democracy." Due to his mobility limitations, the president rode in an open-top car through the facilities while Secret Service agents walked alongside. With Roosevelt in the car are Glenn L. Martin and Nebraska governor Dwight Griswold.

It is important to understand that each aircraft that left Martin-Nebraska had an identity, much like vessels in the Navy. These were ships of the air, and, while the planes were as identical structurally as they could be, their fate and the crews of American boys who filled them were individually unique. The plant workers were not just building trivial household goods. They were building weapons for victory, weapons that in the end made the world a safer place. However, these same aircraft did sometimes serve as funeral pyres for the aircrews aboard. Victory did not come without danger and sacrifice. Because of that, workers made absolutely sure to produce the best quality aircraft, free of any defects.

Efforts had been underway for some time to develop America's atomic weapons program through the Manhattan Project. However, to be used to their fullest potential as a weapon, a delivery system needed to be devised. The United States had no bomber capable of carrying an atomic payload. With the help of Martin-Nebraska, that would soon change, through a project code named Silverplate. (Courtesy of the Library of Congress.)

Col. Paul Tibbets visited Martin-Nebraska at Fort Crook and personally selected 15 B-29s for the undisclosed purpose of carrying an atomic payload. These planes visited the modification plant, where they were altered to meet highly specific standards. Workers recalled the B-29s but had no knowledge of their intended use until after the fact. Two of these B-29s became the *Enola Gay* and the *Bockscar*, the bombers that dropped atomic bombs on Japan. A third B-29 built at Martin-Nebraska, *The Great Artiste*, was the only aircraft to participate in the bombing missions of both Hiroshima and Nagasaki. Utilized to support and document the missions, the plane was eventually heavily damaged and scrapped in 1949.

In 1945, employment numbers were at 13,217 workers. The majority of those, 11,019, worked in the main facility. The remaining 2,198 were employed in the modification center. Over 40 percent of the employees, 5,306, were women, and, while many of them were in clerical and support roles, numerous others were active in the assembly line, working as real-life "Rosie the Riveters."

The last plane to roll off the line at Martin-Nebraska never saw combat or made it into a museum. The plane, 44-86473, one of the Silverplate models customized for an atomic payload, crashed on March 1, 1946, into another B-29 of the 509 Composite Group at Kirtland Army Air Force Base, New Mexico. Less than a year old, it was written off following salvage in April 1946.

Another 765 of the 13,217 workers at Martin-Nebraska were African Americans. Employment at the plant offered a steady job and good pay. One employee, Ralph Orduna, the plant's youngest supervisor, went from constructing planes to piloting them, flying a P-51 with the 332nd Fighter Group, more famously known as the Tuskegee Airmen.

No matter their age, race, or gender, the bittersweet end of their employment came in 1945 for nearly all the employees of Martin-Nebraska. Work had already begun to taper off, and within 30 days of Japan's surrender, many were looking for a new job. In a letter, each employee was given two weeks' notice and thanked for "remaining on the job to final victory."

Bomber 42-24741 saw action with the 497th Bomb Group. Piloted by Lt. W.C. Campbell, the B-29 lost two engines shortly after takeoff from its base in Saipan during a night raid on Osaka in June 1945. Of the men on board, 11 were bailed out and 9 were saved. Today, the remains of 42-24741 are probably somewhere deep in the Pacific Ocean, but its journey began in Nebraska.

The last B-29 came off the assembly line ready to greet the postwar world on September 18, 1945. There had been 10,211 persons employed at the plant on Victory over Japan (V-J) Day. By April 1, 1946, the last 100 workers left Martin-Nebraska. By then, many of the former workers, while proud of their accomplishments, had already melted back into the landscape.

Dismantling of wartime machinery came quickly, and the once-bustling production facility fell silent. In total, 2,116 bombers were produced at the plant, including 1,585 B-26 Marauders and 531 B-29 Superfortresses. Additionally, many B-24s, B-25s, B-26s, and P-40s were reconfigured at the modification plant.

Military operations continued at Fort Crook after the war. Despite the end coming quickly for Martin-Nebraska, its employees, and much of the machinery, it took considerable time, almost two years following the end of the war, for the military to sort out the buildings and war materiel already there. Ultimately, the Second Air Force assumed control of the buildings after consideration was given to keeping them on standby status.

In the fall of 1943, a remodeled post exchange, or PX, opened at Fort Crook. To commemorate the occasion, pictured above, Col. William Mannheimer cut the ribbon at the formal opening on October 28, 1943. Shaking his hand is the commander of the Fort Crook PX, Col. Harry Adamson. In attendance looking on at the ribbon-cutting are, from left to right, Maj. James McGinty, Lt. Col. Frank Ryder, and Maj. Lee Huff Jr., all members of the post exchange council. On any given day, the interior of a typical wartime PX would have been a bustling place. Candy, cigarettes, and other necessities were available to GIs, all at reasonable prices. A bottle of Coca-Cola in 1943 cost a nickel. (Both courtesy of Offutt Air Force Base.)

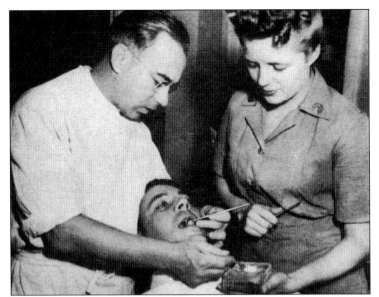

With an army of medical personnel, care at Fort Crook was adequate. Seven additional dentists and numerous Women's Army Corps technicians, including Marjorie Godfrey, assisted Maj. Ivan Kish, the chief of the dental staff at Fort Crook. It was estimated by Kish that between 2,400 and 3,000 fillings were placed at the fort, including one for Pfc. Oscar Mosmeyer.

The holidays can be a difficult time for those in the military. Fortunately, there was no shortage of turkey for Thanksgiving in 1944. A total of 1,500 pounds of turkey and trimmings were prepared for the troops at Fort Crook. Here, from left to right, Cpl. George Bryant, Master Sergeant Gorman, and Private 1st Class Scheuring inspect a batch of turkeys. (Courtesy of Offutt Air Force Base.)

The wartime expansions left an impact on Fort Crook, and helped ensure it remained open after war's end, as the above aerial photograph from 1946 shows. The crisscrossing runways and large bomber facility to the north dwarf the parade ground, once the landmark of the base. In the distance, the budding community of Bellevue still had plenty of lots to fill in. Connecting the foreground and the background, as well as Fort Crook and Omaha, is Fort Crook Road, completed just before the attack on Pearl Harbor. It is a far cry from the postcard of the bomber plant pictured below, which was a common purchase at the PX.

The *Fort Crook Shield* served as the base paper during the war for the 7th Service Command. It included interest articles, notes from the commander's office, chaplain's column, notes from the companies, honor students from the technical schools at Fort Crook, promotions, and more. The 7th Service Command had African American members, and it should be noted that their news and accomplishments were frequently included within the *Shield*.

A World War II–era matchbook from the Fort Crook ordnance depot was presumably not to be used around the ordnance. Uniquely, the oversized matchbook also doubled as a postcard. The translation of the unit insignia, "Nous Les Faisons Rouler," is "We're Rolling." The ordnance depot was deactivated on June 30, 1945. Like the last match in a book, the flame of war burnt itself out and the war ended shortly after.

Four

In Darkening Storms or Sunshine Fair
Strategic Air Command

In the postwar years, Fort Crook underwent a metamorphosis. The fort had been home to Offutt Field since 1924, but on June 12, 1946, the entire installation, while still an Army post, was renamed Offutt Field. The following year, the 131st Army Air Force Base Unit took over housekeeping and administrative duties at Offutt Field. Total manpower strength stood at 71 officers, 674 enlisted men, and 340 civilians.

A Guide to

OFFUTT

AIR FORCE BASE

Fort Crook, Nebraska

APRIL 1948

The year 1948 marks the birth of the United States Air Force. January 13, 1948, is the day the installation was officially redesignated as Offutt Air Force Base and transferred to the Department of the Air Force. In a move that would define the role of the installation for the next 50 years, Offutt AFB was determined to be the new home for Strategic Air Command. The transfer from Andrews Air Force Base took place at one minute past the stroke of midnight on November 9, 1948.

To assist SAC in a multifaceted support role at Offutt, the 3902d Air Base Group had already been activated in late September 1948. Reorganization occurred soon after, and the group became part of the larger 3902d Air Base Wing. Additional units to fall under the command of the new host wing for Offutt included medical and band groups, air police, communications, food service, maintenance, motor vehicle, operations, and supply squadrons.

SAC headquarters was not housed in a massive underground structure complete with a labyrinth of hallways, at least not originally. Instead, it was housed in Building A, a remnant of the Martin-Nebraska facilities. Originally, the building did not even have air conditioning. It was from this modest structure that Gen. Curtis LeMay began his reign as leader of SAC. Today, Building A is still in use as the 55th Wing Law Center.

Under the leadership of LeMay, SAC went from an underappreciated and understaffed force to one of the most respected units in the US military. Upon first assuming command of SAC from his predecessor, Gen. George Kenney, LeMay wrote in a memo, "This afternoon I found a man guarding a hangar with a ham sandwich. There will be no more of that." LeMay had already proven himself during World War II by maximizing the combat efficiency of the B-29 bomber, many of which had been produced at the very same base where he would assume command just a few years later. By the time LeMay left Offutt, SAC's ham sandwich had been replaced with 240,000 airmen, nearly 2,000 bombers, and another 800 tanker aircraft.

LeMay already had quite a reputation by the time he arrived at Offutt. Besides being recognized for his capable leadership abilities, he was also known for his temperament, cigar smoking, and an interest in sports cars. He would serve as the commander in chief of SAC from October 19, 1948, through June 25, 1957. He would go on to serve as the Air Force chief of staff in 1961.

Hot off the presses for the first time on February 24, 1950, the *Air Pulse* newspaper debuted at Offutt. The name of the paper was determined in a contest, with the winner receiving $10. By 1961, the 36-page newspaper had a circulation of 8,000.

Robert Barnes designed the iconic SAC insignia in 1951 during a design contest. The panel of three judges, General LeMay, Gen. Thomas Power, and Brig. Gen. August Kissner, deemed Barnes the winner. He was given a $100 savings bond as a prize. Each feature on the SAC Shield has its own meaning. The new logo replaced a more generic image that shared a closer connection to World War II.

Pres. Harry S. Truman arrived at Offutt on July 16, 1952, at the height of a local crisis. The largest flood in the history of the Missouri River Basin had washed away fields and railroads and flooded over 50 cities. Truman was joined at Offutt by General LeMay and five state governors to discuss the situation. The meeting drew 200 reporters. Truman appealed to the newsmen that "Congress stop fooling around and get something done about these floods."

LeMay's enthusiasm for sports cars led to a feat that would be unimaginable today. The runways were opened for up to 75 sports cars from 19 states for a day at the races—four separate races to be exact—on July 5, 1953. A crowd of 45,000 brought in $56,537, which went towards the Airman's Living Improvement Fund. Car legend Carroll Shelby was the victor of one of the races.

A visitor to Offutt AFB in 1954 would be greeted by a well-dressed, white-peaked-cap-wearing member of the security forces, at that time known as the Air Police. The driver of this Buick Roadmaster, likely an officer, received a smart salute by the air policeman. Members of the Air Police at this time were part of the 3902d. (Courtesy of Mary Langhorst.)

The completed Building 500 was not your typical office building. Instead, it was perhaps the second-most important military building in the country, following the Pentagon. Today, Building 500 is the headquarters for the United States Strategic Command. In several years, following the completion of the new USSTRATCOM building, it is likely that the 55th Wing will relocate its headquarters to the former SAC and USSTRATCOM building.

The SAC underground was built as a product of the Cold War. Despite having three acres of floor space, only three of the seven floors are aboveground. The underground has 24-inch-thick outer walls, while the roof thickness can vary from 24 to 42 inches. When sealed, the underground had its own emergency power system, wells for water, and ample rations to remain operational for an extended period of time.

Archaic by today's standards, the SAC underground command post was the nerve center for America's bomber and missile nuclear operations. Control panels straight out of a science fiction film were adorned with an array of lights and a telephone to connect them to bases over the globe, from Davis-Monthan to Lakenheath to Diego Garcia; they all took their orders from this room at Offutt.

These large maps and charts, known as the "big board," allowed the personnel at SAC headquarters to plot, chart, and track the flight paths of SAC airplanes. SAC was portrayed in two separate films in 1964, the chilling *Fail-Safe*, starring Henry Fonda, and the black comedy *Dr. Strangelove*. Other films include *A Gathering of Eagles* and the Jimmy Stewart film *Strategic Air Command*.

Adequate and fair family housing could sometimes be scarce for a member of the Air Force. To see that the military and their families had proper accommodations, Nebraska senator Kenneth Wherry introduced a bill on March 5, 1949, that alleviated this, allowing for the first 611 units of Wherry housing to be built at Offutt. By the end of 1951, the first military families were already moving into their homes.

At approximately the same time of the Wherry and Capehart housing projects, six "SAC Type" dormitories were built between 1951 and 1956, two of which were initially for the women in the Air Force Program, or "WAF," as an effort to include and increase the role of women.

Further housing was approved at Offutt, and the first 400 units of Capehart housing were constructed in 1956. Like Senator Wherry, Indiana senator Homer Capehart was also a proponent of family military housing. By the 1980s, there were 582 units of Capehart housing for officers and a combined 2,058 units in both Capehart and Wherry for enlisted personnel. The Capehart addition also included the Capehart Chapel, completed in November 1962.

This photograph was taken on July 19, 1955, of a B-25 piloted by T.Sgt. John McKinley (left) after it logged 1,100 hours on both engines, an Offutt record. It was estimated at the time that this was probably one of only 10 B-25s to successfully reach that milestone. Most engines on a B-25 would average between 400 and 600 hours before major maintenance had to be completed.

Construction began on January 22, 1956, on an all-brick chapel with a cost $796,807. On October 6, 1956, the new base chapel was dedicated. Although General LeMay had envisioned several carbon copies of the chapel on other bases, the SAC Memorial Chapel would become one of a kind. At the time of the dedication, Maj. James McConnell was the senior base chaplain, and Catholic, Presbyterian, Lutheran, and Jewish services were all offered.

The unique stained glass of the SAC Memorial Chapel at Offutt depicts an airman with his family and the emblem of Strategic Air Command. With funds raised from donations, the windows were purchased at a cost of $17,000. Eight different firms submitted sketches for the window, but ultimately, Wallis-Wiley Studio of California was chosen, and the windows were dedicated on May 29, 1960.

With God as their copilot, the Chaplain Corps provides a unique role within the military community. The chaplains are available at times of need beyond weekly services and religious education, including funerals and weddings. Today, Offutt offers Catholic, Protestant, Jewish, and Baha'i worship services. The mission of the 55th Wing Chapel is "Providing spiritual care and the opportunity for Airmen, their families, and other authorized personnel to exercise their constitutional right to the free exercise of religion." (Courtesy of Offutt Air Force Base.)

Brig. Gen. James H. Walsh, with (from left to right) Sisters Joan Miriam, Frances Dominic, Joan Michael, and Annunciata met at St. Mary's prior to their tour of Offutt. The sisters were the focus of a *Reader's Digest* story in 1954. The nuns, while not allowed to joyride in the Air Force planes, were honored guests on the general's personal airplane, bringing a literal meaning to the term "flying nun." (Courtesy of Mary Langhorst.)

Because of its proximity to Offutt, the Catholic parish of St. Mary's of Bellevue is home to "Our Lady of the Runways." The nuns would routinely say a prayer for the pilots and crews. In this 1954 photograph, Father Garvey and Sister Mary Otho visit the shrine with a group of children from St. Mary's School. (Courtesy of Mary Langhorst.)

The nuns were not immune to the excitement of meeting the president. During his visit to Offutt on September 29, 1964, Sister Mary Otho (left) and Sister Mary Bede Brown were able to shake hands with Pres. Lyndon B. Johnson. He offered a job well done in his closing remarks after touring the base, as well as a promise to add more to the budget for personnel to receive a pay raise. (Courtesy of Mary Langhorst.)

Following General LeMay's astoundingly lengthy tenure at SAC, his deputy and protégé, Gen. Thomas S. Power, assumed leadership as commander in chief of SAC and was given his fourth star in 1957. Power was at the helm of SAC as America came dangerously close to the brink of nuclear war during the Cuban Missile Crisis. Under orders from Washington, Power entered DEFCON 2, one step away from nuclear war.

The World War II–era runway, intended for medium and heavy bombers of the era, was modified to meet the needs of the growing jet age. In 1958, construction began on the east-west runway to ultimately accommodate the KC-135. Some flight operations were moved to Lincoln Air Force Base during the construction phase. The reconstruction was completed on November 24, 1958, six days ahead of schedule. (Courtesy of Offutt Air Force Base.)

In July 1958, Offutt's first nine-hole golf course was officially opened by General Power. There had already been an apparent interest in golf, as seen in this 1951 photograph during an open house. Trick-shot artist Paul Hahn wallops a 275-yard drive, teeing off from the mouth of Geraldine Elseman, Miss Nebraska 1951. In August 1963, an 18-hole golf course was completed. (Courtesy of Offutt Air Force Base.)

First formed in 1956 at the behest of General LeMay, the SAC Elite Guard, with flashy, unique uniforms that included a chrome, bone-handled .38-caliber revolver and a blue beret, had the chief task of guarding SAC headquarters. The unit also had a drill team until 1969. This particular photograph shows Elite Guard member Omar Svensson (far left), who served in the unit from 1977 to 1979. (Courtesy of Omar Svensson.)

One of the responsibilities and, perhaps, perks of being in the SAC Elite Guard was that during an emergency or even a drill, the SAC Elite Guard had total reign over the halls of the headquarters building. They would run at full speed, shouting, "Clear the halls," and all personnel, including four-star generals, had to hug the walls of the corridors or risk getting knocked down. (Courtesy of Omar Svensson.)

Around June 1959, Staff Sgt. Billy Davis, a member of the SAC Elite Guard, stands watch in front of SAC headquarters at Offutt. Its motto, "Peace is Our Profession," originated in 1957 during a reenlistment drive. It stems from the longer "Maintaining Peace is Our Profession." However, the painter of the sign ran out of room where the slogan was to be, and the shorter saying stuck. (Courtesy of the National Archives and Records Administration.)

Combat Crew, published from 1950 until 1992, served as a monthly publication for SAC. The magazine often featured articles on excellence and efforts. Within the command, Gail Farrell, a veteran of a B-17 crew during World War II and a Korean War veteran from 1950 to 1953, served as an associate editor of *Combat Crew* in a civilian capacity for 22 years, or about 200 issues. (Courtesy of Gail Farrell.)

Under the authorization of Gen. Thomas Power in 1959 and with help from the Air Force and the State of Nebraska, the SAC Museum finally opened in 1966. Adjacent to the base, the museum was a significant draw, averaging 75,000 people each year. In 1998, the museum carefully transported its collection down the road to its new location, halfway between Omaha and Lincoln. With a 300,000-square-foot building, the planes are no longer forced to endure the cold Nebraska winters but can be safely preserved indoors. Known today as the Strategic Air and Space Museum, the aircraft collection includes a B-17, a B-29, a B-52, an EC-135 Looking Glass, a B1 bomber, an SR-71, a U-2, and a Soviet Mig 21.

In 1960, presidential candidate John F. Kennedy visited Offutt to tour SAC headquarters. Pictured with him are chief of staff of the Air Force Gen. Curtis LeMay (center) and Gen. Thomas Power, commander in chief of SAC. Kennedy would again visit in December 1962, just a few short months after the Cuban Missile Crisis.

Lt. Col. Leaford Bearskin was a full-blooded Indian who was proud of his heritage. The decorated World War II and Korean War veteran was known to always keep a headdress in his office. At Offutt, he was squadron commander and assistant headquarters commandant with SAC. He retired from the Air Force at Offutt in 1960 but continued to have a long civilian career with the military. In 1983, he was elected chief of the Wyandotte Nation.

The final 200 units of Capehart housing were completed in October 1963. This 1962 photograph shows that there was still much to be completed in the $27.5 million project, which totaled 414 acres. While Capehart Chapel is visible at lower left, Fort Crook School was still a work in progress. Today, much of the surrounding area has filled in with businesses and further housing.

The ever-popular and talented 702d Air Force Band transferred to Offutt with SAC in 1948, but its lineage can be traced to 1943, when it was the 402d Army Air Forces Band. In 1966, the band reached a new high point, with 60 members. The band has performed on the *Tonight Show* and in numerous college bowl parades, including the Rose Bowl. In 1992, it was redesignated the Heartland of America Band.

In February 1949, Col. Ehrling Bergquist was killed in a plane crash at Offutt. Bergquist had been the first SAC surgeon general at the time of his death. In 1964, a new, state-of-the-art medical facility was constructed at a cost of $4 million. It was dedicated in Bergquist's name and opened on May 7, 1965. Gertrude Bergquist, his widow, and his son Capt. Robert E. Bergquist were both in attendance. Lt. Gen. Kenneth E. Pletcher, the current SAC command surgeon, gave the dedication address. The new hospital opened with 125 beds and boasted that each room included individual thermostats, telephones, television, private bathrooms, and closet space. (Both courtesy of Offutt Air Force Base.)

Gen. John D. Ryan of SAC hosted a visit by Vice Pres. Hubert Humphrey and his wife, Second Lady Muriel Humphrey. The couple was greeted by an honor guard, toured SAC headquarters on May 3, 1965, and received a briefing on the command. General Ryan served as commander in chief of SAC from December 1964 until February 1967.

Lady Bird Johnson, the First Lady of the United States, is seen here wearing an aquamarine dress and holding a bouquet of yellow flowers at Offutt. Mrs. Johnson came to the base in May 1966 as part of her "Keep America Beautiful" campaign. The highpoint of the visit was the planting of an elm tree in front of SAC headquarters. The elm was reportedly a sprig from a tree planted at the White House in 1826 by Pres. John Quincy Adams. (Courtesy of Offutt Air Force Base.)

Ready at a moment's notice, the fire equipment at Offutt, seen above outside the fire station, was unfortunately used from time to time, especially during the heightened activity years of SAC. The P-2 Crash Truck in the foreground could carry both water and foam to quickly put out an aircraft fire. Immediately left of the P-2 is the 23,000-pound 750A Pumper Truck, another common piece of equipment. The fire station was a major improvement from the inadequate original station pictured below. The fire department assisted, and still continues to assist, in nearby communities such as Bellevue and Plattsmouth in the event of extra-alarm emergencies.

Always at the ready, the alert crews were designated flight crews who were housed near the runway. At a moment's notice, they would run to their aircraft and take to the skies as klaxons rang out. The 1960s photograph above demonstrates a crew scrambling from their special alert crew vehicle to board their KC-35 Stratotanker at Offutt. SAC made its goal to get these crews up and flying within 15 minutes of receiving a "go" order from the CINCSAC. The alert crews were essentially on lockdown and not allowed to leave, especially since every second could make the difference between life and death. However, there was always plenty of coffee available in the dining facility.

SAC's responsibilities also included air- and surface-launched guided missiles to accomplish its mission of nuclear deterrence. With sites all over the United States, the missileers of SAC commanded America's arsenal of intercontinental ballistic missiles, but it was again at Offutt where operations were ultimately funneled. An inert Atlas missile and, later, a Minuteman missile stood out front of SAC headquarters.

The 55th Special Reconnaissance Wing moved to Offutt from Forbes Air Force Base in August 1966. In that same time, the 55th SRW was assigned both the RC-135 and the KC-135. The ground and air crews spent countless training hours familiarizing themselves with the new craft. With the new base and new aircraft came a new assignment, Looking Glass Operations.

For 24 hours a day, seven days a week, and 365 days a year for 29 years, Looking Glass Operations remained on constant alert. From 1961 until 1990, an EC-135 was always airborne, serving as a command center in the event of a full-scale nuclear war against the Soviet Union. Command and control could continue in the skies should operations on the ground be obliterated in a nuclear attack. With a full flight crew of 24, the EC-135 Looking Glass was no small operation. By 1987, Looking Glass Operations had been flying for 26 years and accumulated 249,660 hours of flight time.

The 56th secretary of state, Henry Kissinger, visited Offutt to meet with SAC commander Gen. Bruce K. Holloway, who was at Offutt from July 1968 until April 1972. Kissinger served Presidents Nixon and Ford and was a proponent of Vietnamization, a policy that began implementation in 1968 to draw down America's combat role and shift responsibility to South Vietnam. Despite political policy, these were dangerous times for many of the men of SAC. Starting in 1965, B-52 bombers under SAC were brought into direct action during the conflict. Utilized for saturation bombing, they faced enemy fighters and the threat of surface-to-air missiles. A total of 126,615 B-52 sorties took place during the war. SAC reconnaissance planes, including the SR-71 and the U-2, also assumed command of all high-altitude missions over Cambodia, Laos, and North and South Vietnam.

Brig. Gen. Jeanne Holm received a tour of Offutt and the aircraft in 1971. Holm was the first female one-star general in the Air Force and the first female two-star of any branch. Under her initiative, the role of women in the Air Force changed significantly. Holm passed away in 2002 and is buried at Arlington National Cemetery. (Courtesy of Offutt Air Force Base.)

Created following the expansion of the runway in 1971, Base Lake Recreation Area offers over 180 acres to enjoy. The facility includes a stocked freshwater lake, covered picnic shelters, volleyball courts, a basketball court, tent camping sites, and 40 recreational vehicle campsites. A variety of equipment is available for rental during the warm months, including paddle boats, kayaks, and canoes, including the one seen here in April 1987.

Country and gospel singer Tennessee Ernie Ford (front left), known best for his song "Sixteen Tons," sits across from Jim Nabors (front right), better known as Gomer Pyle from the *Andy Griffith Show* and its subsequent spinoff. Both share the picnic table with Gen. Russell Dougherty and his wife. General Dougherty served from August 1974 until 1977. He had risen up through the ranks and was actually a buddy of Pres. Gerald Ford from World War II. They had both been part of a B-29 crew together. As a general, Dougherty had a reputation as being one of the most open and approachable commanders in SAC's history. Following his retirement, the Dougherty Conference Center at Offutt was named in his honor. (Both courtesy of Dorene Sherman.)

A rather serious-looking Pres. Gerald Ford and Gen. John Meyer are seen here as they leave the SAC headquarters checkpoint. Ford, a native son of Nebraska, toured Offutt on February 16, 1974. A decorated fighter pilot during World War II, General Meyer served as commander of SAC from 1972 until his retirement in July 1974. (Courtesy of the Library of Congress.)

Always a supporter of America's men and women in uniform, Bob Hope knew the road to Offutt. Seen here sizing up one of the much-taller SAC Elite Guards, he was an honored guest of Gen. Bennie Davis when Davis was SAC commander in chief. He was also presented with a large commemorative plaque with the shield of SAC on it. Davis served in his position at Offutt from July 1981 until July 1985, prior to his retirement on August 1, 1985.

Bob Hope was not the only one to get the "royal treatment." With short notice, the Queen of England landed at Offutt in 1973. The base quickly moved to provide some proper, albeit low-key, pomp and circumstance when she landed a short time later. After landing, Elizabeth II was greeted by Gen. Bennie Davis and a SAC Elite Guard procession on the runway. The pair toured the underground in SAC and sipped afternoon tea while her Royal Air Force plane was refueled. The press was not permitted at the event, and there was little coverage of the Queen's Nebraska visit.

In the 1970s and early 1980s, Offutt was home to a Royal Air Force (RAF) detachment. The British contingent brought with them the Avro Vulcan strategic bomber, commonly used by the RAF in cooperation with SAC. Below, RAF Air Marshal Kenneth Cross shares what's on his mind with Howard Silber of the *Omaha World Herald* around 1962. (Below, courtesy of Sissy Silber.)

Offutt got in on the bicentennial craze, hosting the Bicentennial Year Armed Forces Day Open House. In the foreground, the 1st Maryland Regiment Colonial Reenactment group marches on parade maneuvers, while several jets can be seen in the background. The July 10–11 event attracted a crowd of 100,000 visitors. (Courtesy of Offutt Air Force Base.)

Little had visibly changed at the main gate between the 1960s and the time this photograph was taken in October 1980. However, the geopolitical scene had changed drastically. From the Cuban Missile Crisis to the warmer détente years of the 1970s, SAC had remained a constant. Now, in the 1980s, global tensions reemerged. Through it all, peace continued as the profession of SAC.

A less remembered fact is a brief visit by the shah of Iran in June 1958. Shah Pahlavi, pictured here wearing his ribbon-filled uniform, was also a guest of President Eisenhower at the White House, despite the State Department classifying his trip as an informal visit. The newly divorced shah may have been more interested in finding a wife than discussing foreign policy. (Courtesy Sissy Silber.)

Believe it or not, cake has been a long-honored tradition for the 55th Wing. The Birthday Ball is a formal event held once a year since 1979 to celebrate the past, present, and future of the 55th Wing. The cake-cutting ceremony includes the oldest ranking member and the youngest airman in attendance. (Courtesy of Offutt Air Force Base.)

Seen here in a unique view looking southwest from inside Offutt's new control tower, the modern tower replaced the World War II–era tower seen in the distance. The new tower offered air traffic controllers an unrestricted view of the runway, hangars, and base operations. (Courtesy of Offutt Air Force Base.)

This aerial view from 1977 shows the might of the 55th Strategic Reconnaissance Wing. Roughly 14,500 officers, enlisted men, and civilian personnel staffed the base at the time. EC-135s, the backbone of the wing, sit on the runway apron, while a pair of E-4s, used for Looking Glass missions, are at the edge. In the foreground is the 2ACCS alert facility, home to Looking Glass Operations. (Courtesy of Offutt Air Force Base.)

Global Shield, first held in 1979, was a training exercise held by SAC to represent a full-scale operation of all its resources, including bombers, reconnaissance, and tanker aircraft. These were major simulations that took place at Offutt and SAC bases worldwide and helped keep the operational readiness at a maximum. (Courtesy of Michael Wagner.)

The "Iron Lady," Margaret Thatcher, visited SAC headquarters when she was prime minister of England in the 1980s, shortly after the Falkland War. It was actually not her first visit to Offutt. In 1967, Thatcher, a young but promising member of parliament, was given her initial tour of the SAC underground. Sir Jeffery Howe, the British foreign secretary from 1983 to 1989, joined her during her second tour. (Courtesy of Dorene Sherman.)

A renovated command post was completed at the SAC underground in 1989. In a blend of fact and fiction, Tom Clancy wrote that "it had been built because Hollywood's rendition of such rooms was better than the one SAC had originally built for itself." In reality, a great deal of technology had changed since the state-of-the-art facility had been built in the 1950s.

One can only imagine what is shown on the monitor as several senior-level officers look at a special display at SAC headquarters in 1988. They are, from left to right, Adm. William Studeman, Gen. William Doyle, and Gen. Lee Butler. Studeman served as director of naval intelligence prior to serving as director of the National Security Agency from 1988 to 1992. (Courtesy of Maj. Gen. William Doyle, USAF Ret.)

Dorene Sherman, the deputy director of protocol at SAC, began her career at Offutt in the 1960s and remained until her retirement in 1999. It was a unique role and a far cry from the Nebraska farm girl life she grew up in. However, similar to many others, Sherman served at Offutt not as a member of the Air Force but as a civilian. Part of her responsibilities included handling special dignitaries during visits, including the author Tom Clancy, who was given access to Offutt to do further research while writing one of his many popular Cold War thrillers. Clancy went on to provide a brief description of Offutt in his Jack Ryan series. (Both courtesy of Dorene Sherman.)

What does one do when the "father of the hydrogen bomb" asks to play the piano? They let him! Dr. Edward Teller was the guest of honor at an event held in the officer's club. A Hungarian Jew, Teller had escaped Nazi Germany and became a naturalized citizen prior to the outbreak of war. Despite this, there are some who claim he was the basis for the character "Dr. Strangelove." (Courtesy of Dorene Sherman.)

Spanning the generations of SAC, Gen. Curtis LeMay and Helen LeMay pose for a photograph with Gen. John Chain Jr. and Judie Chain. General LeMay was of course the first commander in chief of SAC at Offutt, while General Chain was the second-to-last commander in chief of SAC. LeMay passed away at the age of 83 in 1990. General Chain retired from the Air Force in 1991. (Courtesy of Dorene Sherman.)

Pres. George H.W. Bush is seen here with Gen. John Chain Jr., who became the commander in chief of SAC in 1986. President Bush was no stranger to the inside of a cockpit, having been a Navy flier during World War II. While several presidents have visited Offutt, Bush seemed to genuinely enjoy the experience. It was under President Bush that SAC was taken off 24-hour-alert status in 1991. It then stood down the following year, in 1992. Replacing General Chain, Gen. Lee Butler served as the last commander of SAC, as well as the first commander of USSTRATCOM.

Five

ON THE FRONTIER
BEYOND THE COLD WAR

The insignia that was once recognized as the shield of America's national security and nuclear deterrence suddenly became an item destined for museums and the basements of retirees. In a formal ceremony, the legendary SAC emblem was retired on June 1, 1992. The ceremony was officiated by Gen. Colin Powell, a member of the joint chiefs of staff. The same ceremony also marked the establishment of USSTRATCOM. (Courtesy of Dorene Sherman.)

With the easing of Cold War tensions, a Russian delegation visited Offutt. During the SAC years, this would have been unimaginable. However, this visit was following the drawdown of SAC and the establishment of USSTRATCOM. Parked on the runway for viewing, a somewhat archaic Russian Tupolev bomber sits next to an American B-52 Stratofortress. The two nations entered into the Open Skies Treaty following the Cold War. The treaty permitted unarmed aerial reconnaissance over treaty participants' territory in an effort to share a mutual understanding pertaining to military efforts. The American aircraft tasked for this use, a trio of OC-135s, were stationed at Offutt and assigned to the 55th Wing. (Both courtesy of Dorene Sherman.)

The Air Force Weather Agency (AFWA) has called Offutt home since 1997, though it can trace its lineage to World War I. AFWA's mission is to "maximize America's power through the exploitation of timely, accurate, and relevant weather information; anytime, everywhere." Serving under AWFA, the 1st Weather Group, headquartered at Offutt, aids in weather-related duties to Air Force, Army, National Guard, and Army Reserve units at 350 installations throughout the continental United States. The Thomas S. Moorman Building, the AFWA headquarters, was dedicated in 2008 and utilizes modern architectural advancements to ensure that the building is energy efficient and environmental LEED–certified. (Both courtesy of Offutt Air Force Base.)

Every year, the Defenders of Freedom Open House and Air Show attracts thousands of members of the general public to the normally restricted-access base. A major logistics and security challenge, the Air Force coordinates carefully with several volunteer organizations, including the Air Force Association, to have a successful event year after year. The two-day, free-admission event usually combines a mix of current aircraft and stationary exhibits that visitors can walk through, as well as numerous vintage aircraft. The Blue Angels, Thunderbirds, and Golden Knights parachute teams have all participated in the airshow. (Both US Air Force photographs, by Josh Plueger.)

The post cemetery dates back to the old Fort Crook days. Today, it sits in a quiet corner of the base. The first burial there occurred in 1897 and was actually a civilian from the nearby town. A number of Spanish-American War veterans are buried there, following losing battles with tropical disease. Sadly, a large number of graves are filled by children and spouses, a demonstration that the sacrifice and commitment of military life can often extend to the families of men and women in uniform. Every Memorial Day, a service is held at the now-full post cemetery in remembrance of the contributions of those who have served, and continue to serve, this nation. (Above, courtesy of John Daly; below, US Air Force photograph, by Josh Plueger.)

Pres. George W. Bush and First Lady Laura Bush, along with former New York mayor Rudy Giuliani and his wife, Judith, visited Offutt in 2004. They are seen here being greeted by Brig. Gen. John Koziol, commander, and Col. John Daly, vice commander, 55th Wing. The visit marked a return trip for President Bush. Concerned about the possibility of the White House being a target, Air Force One flew to Offutt on September 11, 2001, following the terrorist attacks. (Courtesy of John Daly.)

Offutt has an attachment to the Sarpy County community, particularly Bellevue. Here, from left to right, Brig. Gen. James Jones, commander of the 55th Wing, along with Col. Rob Maness, 55th Wing vice commander, and command C.M. Sgt. Lisa Sirois, march down Mission Avenue in Olde Towne Bellevue during the 2008 Veterans' Day parade, held annually since 2000. (US Air Force photograph, by Josh Plueger.)

A crane moves a section of the old control tower while the new, much larger control tower looms over the remains of the former tower. By the end of the day, the old tower was completely removed. A ribbon cutting was held for the modern control tower on May 9, 2007. (US Air Force photograph, by Josh Plueger.)

A T-38 Talon makes a very low pass over the parade ground at Offutt. The T-38 is not usually thought of as an aircraft of the 55th Wing, but it was assigned to the wing for several years during the early 1990s. The jet trainer allowed pilots the continued opportunity to gain further flying time. The Tail Code "OF" is specially designated for Offutt Air Force Base.

T. Sgt. Al Kremer (far right) leads a flight of Offutt Air Force Base airmen in a parade in downtown Omaha in 1953. In 1968, he retired from the Air Force, but returned to Offutt six months later as a civilian working for SAC. Years later, after SAC stepped down and USSTRATCOM stepped up, Al Kremer remained. He worked for 12 SAC commanders, beginning with General LeMay, and six USSTRATCOM commanders. By the time Kremer retired, on January 19, 2007, he had a combined 60 years of service as a military member and civilian employee. (Both courtesy of Offutt Air Force Base.)

In July 2007, the space shuttle *Atlantis* arrived at Offutt, affixed to a NASA 747. Following a mission to the International Space Station, the craft was being returned from California to the Kennedy Space Center in Florida when it was forced to detour to Offutt due to bad weather. The event marked the second and final time Offutt was visited by a space shuttle.

Dignitaries, including the mayor of Bellevue, the governor of Nebraska, and congressmen and senators, joined Gen. C. Robert Kehler and members of the Department of Defense in a formal ground-breaking of the new USSTRATCOM building. The new facility is on the site of the former nine-hole golf course. The 915,876-square-foot, $524.4 million facility will allow USSTRATCOM to more effectively accomplish its mission. (Photograph by Steve Cunningham.)

Visible from the air, this message carved into the crops just south of Offutt is a small way the local community thanks the Offutt community. For the last several years, this farmer has created several different messages with the help of GPS and many bags of flour to spell out the lettering.

Employees from area Wal-Mart stores donate their time to help create the giant message, measuring 3,990 feet long. Reportedly, there is a framed photograph of the message at both the White House and Pentagon. (Courtesy Bellevue Wal-Mart Supercenter)

BIBLIOGRAPHY

Cencich, JR. *A Chronology of Offutt Air Force Base*. Offutt Air Force Base: Dept. of the Air Force, 1962.

Del Papa, Michael E. *Strategic Air Command Missile Chronology: 1939–1973*. Offutt Air Force Base: Office of the Historian, Headquarters Strategic Air Command, 1975.

Hansen, A.I. *The History of Fort Crook 1888–Offutt Air Force Base 1976*. Offutt Air Force Base: Dept. of the Air Force, 1976.

History of Generals' Row. Offutt Air Force Base: Dept. of the Air Force, 1979.

History of the 3902d Air Base Wing. Offutt Air Force Base: Dept. of the Air Force, 1982.

Mitchell, Lawrence A. *The Aircraft History of the 55th Strategic Reconnaissance Wing*. Offutt Air Force Base: Dept. of the Air Force, 1988.

Offutt Air Force Base. San Diego, CA: Marcoa Publishing, 1995.

Simmons, Jerold L., ed. *"La Belle Vue" Studies in the History of Bellevue, Nebraska*. Marceline, MO: Walsworth Publishing Company, 1976.

ABOUT THE SARPY COUNTY MUSEUM

Located at 2402 Clay Street in Bellevue, the Sarpy County Museum is dedicated to protecting, promoting, and preserving the history of Sarpy County, its communities, and their people. Dating back to 1934, the organization serves as "the Smithsonian of Sarpy County." Staff and volunteers serve as docents, work with collections, prepare displays, facilitate programs, and ensure that the rich history of Sarpy County does not fade away.

The museum features several rotating exhibitions to augment the permanent displays, one of which is of particular relevance to this book, an interactive scale model of Fort Crook in 1937 prior to its drastic transformation during the onset of World War II. The collection includes artifacts, government records, newspapers, historical documents, photographs, and a variety of other resources, all available to the public. Rather than leave it in the attic or basement, the museum strongly encourages people to share anything that might be historically or culturally significant to Sarpy County.

Additionally, several historical properties, including Bellevue's historic Log Cabin, the Chicago, Burlington & Quincy railroad depot, and the Moses Merill Mission site are affiliated with the museum. The cabin and depot have been preserved to nearly their original condition. All sites are available for tours.

Primary support to fund these endeavors comes from Sarpy County, grants, fundraisers, memberships, and donations from readers. As a small, nonprofit 501(c)3 organization with a big mission, it is through these financial efforts that the museum can continue to save local history.

The Sarpy County Museum is on Facebook and Twitter and can be contacted at 402-292-1880 or info@sarpycountymuseum.org. The museum is open Tuesday through Sunday from 10:00 a.m. to 4:00 p.m. We hope to see you soon!

DISCOVER THOUSANDS OF LOCAL HISTORY BOOKS FEATURING MILLIONS OF VINTAGE IMAGES

Arcadia Publishing, the leading local history publisher in the United States, is committed to making history accessible and meaningful through publishing books that celebrate and preserve the heritage of America's people and places.

Find more books like this at
www.arcadiapublishing.com

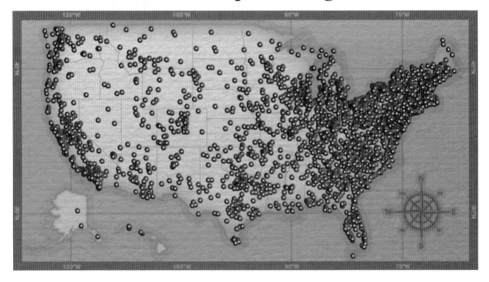

Search for your hometown history, your old stomping grounds, and even your favorite sports team.

Consistent with our mission to preserve history on a local level, this book was printed in South Carolina on American-made paper and manufactured entirely in the United States. Products carrying the accredited Forest Stewardship Council (FSC) label are printed on 100 percent FSC-certified paper.

MADE IN THE